BLUEBELL RAILWAY

Sixty Years of Progress 1960–2020

Colin Tyson

AMBERLEY

Front Cover: SECR O1 No. 65 passes the bluebells in Lindfield Wood with the 2.45 p.m. train from Sheffield Park on 5 May 2018. (Peter Edwards)

Back Cover: The desolate scene at Sheffield Park station that awaited the visit of the first committee members in 1959.

All photographs, Bluebell Railway Archive, unless stated.

First published 2020

Amberley Publishing
The Hill, Stroud
Gloucestershire, GL5 4EP

www.amberley-books.com

British Library Cataloguing in Publication Data.
A catalogue record for this book is available from the British Library.

ISBN 978 1 4456 8842 8 (print)
ISBN 978 1 4456 8843 5 (ebook)

Typesetting and Origination by Amberley Publishing.
Printed in Great Britain.

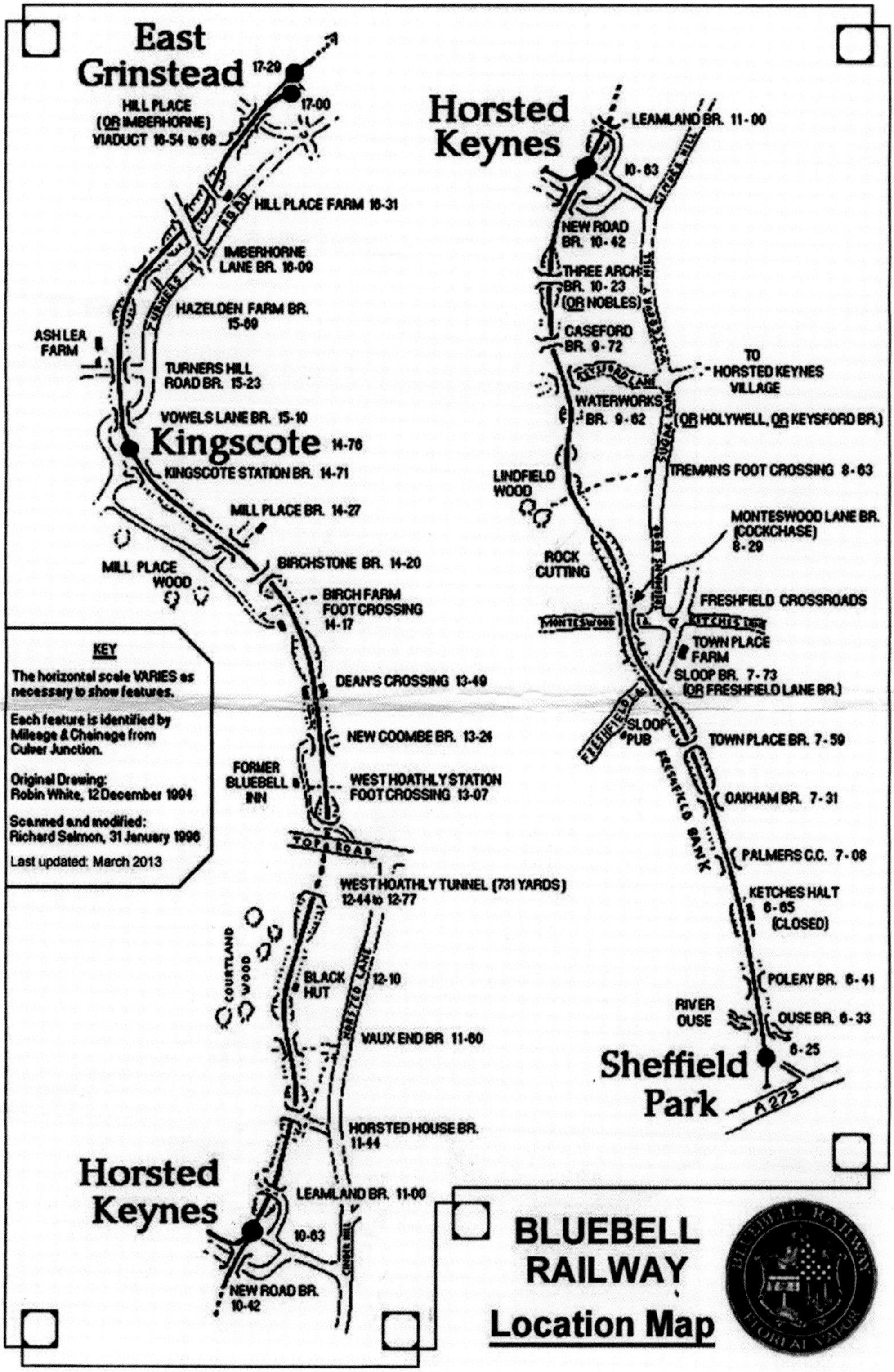
East Grinstead 17-29
17-00
HILL PLACE (OR IMBERHORNE) VIADUCT 16-54 to 68
ROAD
HILL PLACE FARM 16-31
IMBERHORNE LANE BR. 16-09
TURNERS HILL
HAZELDEN FARM BR. 15-69
ASH LEA FARM
TURNERS HILL ROAD BR. 15-23
VOWELS LANE BR. 15-10
Kingscote 14-76
KINGSCOTE STATION BR. 14-71
MILL PLACE BR. 14-27
MILL PLACE WOOD
BIRCHSTONE BR. 14-20
BIRCH FARM FOOT CROSSING 14-17
KEY
The horizontal scale VARIES as necessary to show features.
Each feature is identified by Mileage & Chainage from Culver Junction.
Original Drawing: Robin White, 12 December 1994
Scanned and modified: Richard Salmon, 31 January 1996
Last updated: March 2013
DEAN'S CROSSING 13-49
NEW COOMBE BR. 13-24
FORMER BLUEBELL INN
WEST HOATHLY STATION FOOT CROSSING 13-07
TOP ROAD
WEST HOATHLY TUNNEL (731 YARDS) 12-44 to 12-77
COURTLAND WOOD
BLACK HUT 12-10
HORSTED LANE
VAUX END BR 11-60
HORSTED HOUSE BR. 11-44
Horsted Keynes
LEAMLAND BR. 11-00
10-63
CINDER HILL
NEW ROAD BR. 10-42
Horsted Keynes
LEAMLAND BR. 11-00
10-63
CINDER HILL
NEW ROAD BR. 10-42
THREE ARCH BR. 10-23 (OR NOBLES)
CASEFORD BR. 9-72
TREEMANS ROAD
KEYSFORD LANE
TO HORSTED KEYNES VILLAGE
WATERWORKS BR. 9-62
(OR HOLYWELL, OR KEYSFORD BR.)
SUGAR LANE
LINDFIELD WOOD
TREMAINS FOOT CROSSING 8-63
MONTESWOOD LANE BR. (COCKCHASE) 8-29
ROCK CUTTING
FRESHFIELD CROSSROADS
MONTESWOOD
KETCHES LANE
TOWN PLACE FARM
SLOOP BR. 7-73 (OR FRESHFIELD LANE BR.)
FRESHFIELD LANE
SLOOP PUB
TOWN PLACE BR. 7-59
FRESHFIELD BANK
OAKHAM BR. 7-31
PALMERS C.C. 7-08
KETCHES HALT 6-65 (CLOSED)
POLEAY BR. 6-41
RIVER OUSE
OUSE BR. 6-33
6-25
Sheffield Park
A 275
BLUEBELL RAILWAY
Location Map
BLUEBELL RAILWAY
FLOREAT VAPOR

Introduction

The Bluebell Railway, as we know it today in its preserved form, started life as part of the Lewes & East Grinstead Railway, connecting the two Sussex market towns with the rest of the railway network of the time. The principal backer was Henry North Holroyd, the 3rd Earl of Sheffield, resident at Sheffield Park, who chaired a meeting on Saturday 30 September 1876 at the Star Hotel, Lewes, of local landowners and promoters to consider the practicality of such a scheme. Present was Mr John Wolfe Barry, who was to become the line's engineer.

This was at a time of great 'railway mania', with plenty of schemes for new lines being proposed, many of which being subsequently rejected. However, the Bill for the railway south from East Grinstead, together with a branch from Horsted Keynes to Copyhold on the Brighton main line, was eventually deposited and an Act of Parliament authorised in 1877. The original intention of the promoters had been to continue their line towards London from East Grinstead, which had not been built at that time. The nearest access to the main London to Brighton line was via the line already built to Three Bridges from Tunbridge Wells, which passed through East Grinstead.

Many independently promoted lines in Sussex eventually became part of the London, Brighton & South Coast Railway prior to their completion, usually because the promoter's finances had run out but primarily to secure and facilitate the transmission of traffic. In reality, it was the Brighton company's contractor, Joseph Firbank, who was tasked with construction of the line, having previously built the line from Shoreham to Horsham and the Pulborough to Arundel section of the Mid-Sussex line.

The first navvies arrived in August 1878 and the line was progressively built to include the major infrastructure items of a 731-yard tunnel at West Hoathly and a 262-yard viaduct at Imberhorne on the approach to East Grinstead. After much delay, the line duly opened to public traffic on 1 August 1882, branching off the Lewes to Uckfield line at Culver Junction and with stations at Barcombe Cross, Newick & Chailey, Fletching (Sheffield Park), Horsted Keynes, West Hoathly, Kingscote and East Grinstead. The line from Horsted Keynes to Copyhold Junction on the London to Brighton main line opened a year later, on 3 September 1883.

One of the people to travel on the first Up train over the line was seven-year-old Miss Kate Longley of Selsfield Place, Turners Hill, who travelled with her family from Kingscote to East Grinstead and back. She made history seventy-eight years later by also travelling on the first train at the opening of the Bluebell Railway on 7 August 1960.

Timber sawmills at Sheffield Park and Kingscote and an adjacent dairy at Sheffield Park provided goods traffic in the pre-war years and larger goods trains frequently used this diversionary route from the main Brighton line, at least until the Quarry Line was built and the quadrupling of the main line to Balcombe Tunnel. Passenger services were adequate for the demand and the rural line lived 'under the radar' for most of its life through LBSCR, Southern Railway (1923–48) and early British Railways ownership. But the economic tide had already turned...

Pre-1959

Rationalisation of the line's signalling system had already been carried out by the Southern Railway and the increasing effects of the motor bus and lorry, which could deliver passengers and goods virtually door-to-door, were no match for the rural railway, with its inconveniently placed stations – only the intermediate stations of Barcombe and West Hoathly being situated close to the local population. The line's fortunes continued to plummet during the late 1940s and early 1950s, not helped by a slow and infrequent passenger service that was pretty much unchanged since the outset – eight trains each way on weekdays and two on Sundays.

In 1954 British Railways proposed the closure of the line, with the date set for 28 May 1955. Closure was originally scheduled for 13 June 1955 but an ASLEF strike brought the line to a premature close.

The local press had caught on to the 'Bluebell' name after a resident suggested the trains were slow enough to get out and pick bluebells, although enginemen and railway staff had also used the nickname 'Bluebell and Primrose Line' to describe the line.

But BR had reckoned without local Chailey resident Miss Rose Ellen Margaret (Madge) Bessemer – chair of the fighting committee against closure of the line. She had spotted a flaw in the closure procedures followed by the British Transport Commission: the Act of Parliament that had authorised the opening of the line had not been repealed through subsequent ownerships to provide four trains a day each way – and closure was therefore illegal. The discovery proved a sensation and the press lapped it up.

The Bluebell 'Victory' headboard is adjusted by a member of the station staff at East Grinstead, prior to No. 80154 shunting across to the Down platform, where almost a thousand people wait to board the last train to Lewes on 16 March 1958.

BR reluctantly began running trains again from 7 August 1956 and Miss Bessemer was besieged as a celebrity by the press on the first train. BR replied by acting in the spirit of the original Act of Parliament by just providing four trains a day at inconvenient times for either work or leisure purposes, which was dubbed 'The Sulky Service'. This service was only required to stop at the stations mentioned in the original Act – Newick & Chailey, Sheffield Park, Horsted Keynes and West Hoathly.

In March 1957 a Bill was presented to Parliament by the BTC to repeal the original 1878 Act. This meant that they could now close the line legally and, following a three-day public inquiry, it was announced that the last trains would run for the second and final time on 16 March 1958. The final trip of the day, the late-running 4.28 p.m. departure from East Grinstead, saw three extra coaches added to the six-coach formation amid much fanfare.

Thankfully, BR did not immediately tear up the track after final services and the route through Ardingly, Horsted Keynes and East Grinstead was still used for some trains of condemned wagons and Race Specials from Brighton to Lingfield.

1959

Meanwhile, four Brighton students, Chris Campbell, David Dallimore, Martin Eastland and Alan Sturt, arranged for local enthusiast and professional railwayman Bernard Holden to chair an initial meeting to form the Lewes & East Grinstead Railway Preservation Society. This meeting, open to all those interested in running the line privately (utilising a GWR diesel railcar!), was held on 15 March at the Church Lads'

A staged mock-up of the society's first meeting on 15 March 1959 at Haywards Heath, taken as part of a TV documentary made in 1964.

Brigade Hall in Haywards Heath. A committee was chosen and subscriptions taken at that meeting.

A further committee meeting held at the same location on 1 June changed the name to the 'shortened' Bluebell Railway Preservation Society – a name that had now 'stuck' – and concentrated its efforts on the section from Sheffield Park, where there was readily available water for engines, to Horsted Keynes. The connection to the outside world from Horsted Keynes to Haywards Heath was to prove invaluable in bringing redundant engines and rolling stock to the line.

The newly formed committee paid a visit to Sheffield Park in June and BR was asking for £34,000 for the 4.8-mile section. The society had £89 in the bank! A five-year lease on the line was later arranged with BR in order to gain some breathing space to raise funds.

On 12 July the society ran its first fund-raising railtour, starting at Tonbridge, to East Grinstead and down to Horsted Keynes, where the society chairman addressed the audience before the train continued via Haywards Heath and Lewes back to Tonbridge. The society had 400 members 'and it was hoped to increase this to 1,000'.

This was followed on 27 September by a 'Rally Day' at Sheffield Park station, at which a pump trolley was used to demonstrate the recently reinstated signalling equipment.

The committee entering Sheffield Park station in June 1959.

Bereft of name and with grass growing high on the track.

Volunteers clearing the track of weeds – by hand!

Bluebell's first railtour, from Tonbridge to Horsted Keynes, passes West Hoathly with No. 32535 on 12 July 1959.

A pump trolley is used to demonstrate the commissioning of signalling on Rally Day, 27 September 1959.

The four founding students that called the first meeting to save the 'Bluebell Line' at a reunion in 2004. From left to right: David Dallimore, Alan Sturt, Chris Campbell and Marin Eastland with (centre) society chairman Roy Watts. Alan and Martin have since passed away.

1960

Membership rises to 600 and at a meeting held at Brighton Pavilion on 19 February, a gathering of 200 members are told that the five-year lease will not become operative until a Light Railway Order is granted. Rolling stock needed to be acquired, a halt needed to be constructed at New Road, Horsted Keynes, for trains to terminate a few hundred yards south of the BR station, and a loco shed and inspection pit needed to be built.

On 7 May the BRPS acquired its first locomotive, LBSCR No. 55 *Stepney*, arriving from Brighton under its own steam at Horsted Keynes, together with LSWR Third No. S320 and Maunsell Brake No. S6575 – these two coaches formed the entire passenger fleet for the 1960 season. SECR P Class No. 323 arrived on 27 June, enabling a push-pull formation train to be operated.

The Ministry of Transport Inspection took place on 9 July and was passed with flying colours to enable a Light Railway Order.

The railway states its presence in this rare view of the overbridge on the A275 south of Sheffield Park station prior to demolition.

A makeshift terminus was constructed just south of Horsted Keynes station for Bluebell trains prior to the official opening of the line.

The railway's first locomotive, LBSCR No. 55 *Stepney*, passes through Ardingly under its own steam from Brighton to Horsted Keynes, together with LSWR Third No. S320 and Maunsell Brake No. S6575 on 7 May 1959.

A chalked notice declares the train times for opening day, Sunday 7 August 1960.

Crowds line the platforms at Sheffield Park to witness *Stepney* depart on opening day, 7 August. No. 323 is at the rear of the two-coach train. Note the TV cameraman on top of the platform canopy.

No. 323 stands at Sheffield Park on 18 August 1960. (R. C. Riley)

Thus the Bluebell Railway was formally opened on 7 August with more than 2,000 people present at Sheffield Park, along with press and TV cameras. A major landmark in British railway history had been achieved.

Fletcher Jennings industrial locomotive *Captain Baxter* arrived at the railway on 15 August, having spent its entire life at the Dorking Greystone Limestone Works at Betchworth, Surrey.

At the end of the year 12,000 people had travelled on the line, gross receipts exceeded £2,000 and membership stood at more than 1,500.

1961

The 1961 season was boosted on 2 March by the arrival of the 'Chesham' coaches – four close-coupled former Metropolitan Line's Chesham branch carriages were purchased from London Transport at a cost of £65 each and immediately entered service.

The season started on 1 April and, with the recently arrived SECR No. 27 *Primrose*, trains ran with *Stepney* and *Primrose* at the front and *Bluebell* at the rear, behind the four new coaches.

On 22 April a second BRPS railtour ran from Brighton to Horsted Keynes via Steyning, Horsham, Three Bridges, East Grinstead, Oxted and the Cuckoo Line to Polegate, then on to Lewes and Horsted Keynes via Ardingly. Motive power included E6 No. 32418, and E4 class Nos 32505, 32479 and 32564.

An appeal for funding is launched to secure North London Railway No. 55850 and LSWR Adams Radial tank No. 30583. The Adams arrived on 12 July, coming in steam from Brighton via Ardingly.

From 29 October the Bluebell is finally given access to Horsted Keynes station by BR, sharing the station with the electric service from Haywards Heath that uses the westernmost platform.

The railway attracted its first film contract – *The Innocents*, starring Deborah Kerr.

92,000 passengers were carried in 1961.

No. 323 *Bluebell* and No. 55 *Stepney* (now painted in LBSCR livery) on the first running day of the 1961 season, 1 April. (R. C. Riley)

No. 323 *Bluebell* arrives at Sheffield Park with a Down train on the first day of the 1961 season with the four newly acquired Chesham coaches.

The second BRPS railtour passes Polegate on 22 April 1961.

The railway's first film contract, *The Innocents*, in 1961, starred Deborah Kerr, seen here plugging her ears as the safety valves lift on No. 323 *Bluebell.*

1962

The scene at Sheffield Park had now changed with the arrival of a buffet car and two carriages for catering parked in the dock road, with seats for up to 200 people and some tables and chairs outside and 'light lunches' now available from volunteer staff.

GWR 'Dukedog' class No. 9017 *Earl of Berkeley* arrived on 15 February as the railway's first tender locomotive. At the time it was saved for preservation, Bluebell was the only line where it could run.

A month later, on 28 March, came an ex-North London Railway 0-6-0T goods engine carrying its LNWR livery of No. 2650.

On 1 April a special train left London Bridge for Sheffield Park via Ardingly, hauled by Captain Bill Smith's preserved GNR J52 class No. 1247. The infamous Dr Beeching joined the train at Three Bridges and later 'officially opened' Holywell (Waterworks) Halt, constructed at this location by the society because it was on a bus route.

LBSCR E4 class No. 473 *Birch Grove* arrived at the line on 16 October, named by the 'Brighton' after a hamlet close to Horsted Keynes.

Santa Specials are now an important revenue-earning period for all heritage railways, but the very first standard gauge 'Santa Special' was on Boxing Day 1962 with Santa in his seasonally decorated brake van.

The new arrivals of 1962 stand at Sheffield Park: GWR No. 9017 and NLR No. 2650. The original 1960-built locomotive shed, which housed two locomotives, stands behind.

Preserved GNR J52 class No. 1247 at Sheffield Park on 1 April 1962. (R. C. Riley)

Britain's first standard gauge 'Santa Special' – Boxing Day 1962, with Santa in his seasonally decorated brake van.

1963

The LNWR Observation Car arrived at Sheffield Park on 24 February and has proved popular with visitors ever since, due to its large viewing windows. It formerly worked on the Conwy Valley Line from Llandudno to Blaenau Ffestiniog in North Wales.

The 'Spring Belle' rail tour came to Sheffield Park from London on 31 March, hauled by BR Standard 4 tank No. 80084 and No. 473 *Birch Grove*. Caledonian Railway 4-2-2

BR Standard 4 tank No. 80084 and No. 473 *Birch Grove* arrive at Haywards Heath after a spirited run from East Croydon on 31 March 1963.

The 'Caledonian Blue Belle' Special waits to leave Victoria on 15 September 1963.

No. 123 was brought down from Scotland to haul the 'Caledonian Blue Belle' railtour of 15 September with LSWR T9 No. 120. Adams Radial No. 488 and No. 473 *Birch Grove* were coupled to the rear of the train at Haywards Heath and at Horsted Keynes No. 27 took over for the run to Sheffield Park.

28 October saw the last day of BR train services on the Ardingly branch. This final day saw *Stepney* and *Birch Grove* travel via the line to Brighton for servicing before forming a 'special' named the 'Brighton Blue Belle' to Sheffield Park and back. The two engines travelled light back to Sheffield Park that evening.

The Revd W. Awdry published *Stepney the Bluebell Engine* as one of a series of his successful Thomas the Tank Engine children's books.

Adams Radial No. 488 and No. 473 *Birch Grove* light engine at Haywards Heath in connection with the railtour of 15 September 1963. (R. C. Riley)

Crowds at Ardingly on the last day of service as the 'Brighton Blue Belle' leaves for Horsted Keynes.

1964

Industrial Aveling & Porter 'traction engine on rails' locomotive *The Blue Circle* arrived at Sheffield Park on 23 April. Underpowered for the line's needs, it did haul the observation car up Freshfield Bank twice in October 1964.

The first 'Bluebell on Parade' event was held on Sunday 21 June, followed by a second on 16 August. A Vintage Transport Weekend was held on 17–18 October. These two events continued to form the basis of the special event calendar right into the late 1970s.

The overbridge on the A275 at Sheffield Park is demolished, severing the route of the former trackbed south to Lewes.

North London Railway No. 2650 and later No. 473 *Birch Grove* are hired by BR contractors to help lift redundant track between Ardingly and Hortsed Keynes and from there to West Hoathly, following failure of the contractor's petrol loco. The remaining line from Copyhold to Ardingly is singled to serve a roadstone depot.

Aveling & Porter No. 9449 *The Blue Circle* was presented to the railway in 1964 by its owners, Associated Portland Cement.

No. 473 *Birch Grove* leased to contractors for tracklifting duty near Lywood Tunnel, Ardingly, in August 1964.

1965

The first and only non-steam engine for many years to come arrived in March in the shape of Howard of Bedford shunting locomotive No. 957 *Britannia*. Coupled to a wagon with a boom, it finds a useful role in hauling weed-killing trains.

GWR No. 3217 *Earl of Berkeley* entered service on 13 June, followed by the arrival of the LBSCR Directors' Saloon on 4 August.

The line's fifth anniversary was celebrated on 8 August with a re-enactment of the 1960 first train formation.

Howard shunting locomotive No. 957 *Britannia* is ready to travel up the line on weed-killing duties.

GWR No. 3217 *Earl of Berkeley* and coach No. 1061 both entered service on 13 June 1965.

1966

A milestone was reached on 4 September when Miss Sue Blanchard became the millionth passenger to travel the line. On this occasion No. 323 *Bluebell* is unveiled in her new 'Bluebell Blue' lined livery by TV celebrity Richard Hearne (aka Mr Pastry).

A 'Line Purchase Appeal' is launched for funds to help secure the freehold of the line.

TV's 'Mr Pastry' with BRPS President Bishop Geoffrey Warde at the unveiling of *Bluebell*'s new livery.

No. 323 *Bluebell* sporting her new livery in 1966.

1967

The former Bluebell Line stations at Newick & Chailey and West Hoathly are demolished.

A large film contract for the time, *I'll Never Forget What's Is Name* saw a makeshift building added to what was left of Bluebell Halt and the North London Tank and the Chesham set of coaches painted completely white.

9 July saw the end of steam on Southern Region routes from Waterloo on the Bournemouth and Salisbury lines, making the Bluebell uniquely steam-hauled in the south of England.

The first station south of Sheffield Park, Newick & Chailey, was demolished in 1967.

A whitewashed North London Railway loco bears down on the classic 'damsel in distress' for filming *I'll Never Forget What's Is Name.*

End of Southern steam: the last Channel Island boat train at Waterloo on 8 July 1967. (John Sharp Collection)

1968

11 August 1968 saw the last main-line passenger train to be hauled by steam on BR with the running of the famous 'Fifteen Guinea Special' in the north-west of England. By this time, the 'unique' Bluebell had been joined by other early preserved railway schemes across the UK, including the Dart Valley Railway, Severn Valley Railway and the Keighley & Worth Valley Railway.

More importantly, down in Sussex, the Bluebell had secured its future with completion of the purchase of the line from BR. A ceremony was held at Sheffield Park on 27 October with the handing over of a framed scroll. For the price of £43,500, the railway now owned the 5-mile line from Sheffield Park to Horsted Keynes plus the stations, yards and ten railway cottage dwellings.

The line purchase would not have been possible without the many schemes such as 'Pennies on the Line', members' loans and general box rattling from our 1960s General Manager Horace May. He is pictured here with two famous society members – stars of TV, radio and stage Elsie and Doris Waters. Chairman John Leroy stands on the left.

The handing over of a commemorative parchment by Frank Harrison, Divisional Manager, Central Division, Southern Region, at the line purchase ceremony on 27 October 1968.

1969

The year started with the arrival on 22 January of BR Standard Class 4 locomotive No. 75027, which had been withdrawn from Carnforth and purchased anonymously (at the time) by the late member Charlie Pyne. It appeared to be a far larger loco than was necessary for Bluebell in the late 1960s but soon proved its worth into the 1970s and beyond.

The BRPS celebrated its tenth year since its founding.

All through the 1960s, the repair and painting of the railway's carriage stock had to be undertaken in the open air, both in the dock roads at Sheffield Park and at Horsted Keynes. The coach being worked on here is SER Composite No. 1050.

1970

A third ex-SECR P class locomotive, No. 178, arrives at the railway, initially as a donor engine for its other two stablemates.

A small extension is added to the original engine shed and a Tenth Anniversary Appeal is launched to fund a new fourteen-coach carriage shed at Horsted Keynes.

The early 1970s see an influx of new rolling stock, following the economy years of saving surplus funds to purchase the line. SR Bulleid Open Third No. 1481 and Saloon Third Brake No. 4279 came in July 1970. A month later, on 16 August, came SECR C class No. 592, owned by the Wainwright 'C' Preservation Society, which had been preserved in the old running shed at Ashford since 1966.

A young Elton John uses Sheffield Park station as the backdrop to his third album *Tumbleweed Connection.*

The third SECR P class locomotive to come to Bluebell was No. 178, seen here when named *Pioneer II* and on loan by BR to Bowaters of Sittingbourne. (Gavin Morrison)

SR Saloon Third Brake No. 4279 arrives at Sheffield Park on 9 July 1970.

1971

Erection of a new four-road carriage shed starts at Horsted Keynes, funded by members and supporters.

The preservation scheme at Hampshire's Longmoor Military Railway fails – the Bulleid Society and the Southern Loco Preservation Co. start moving their initial stock to the Bluebell, starting with Bulleid West Country Pacific No. 21C123 *Blackmoor Vale* on 29 September and ex-Southampton Dock Shunter SR 'USA' class No. 30064 on 24 October.

An ex-LMS sleeping car comes to Sheffield Park to provide overnight volunteer accommodation.

The privately owned Great Northern Railway Directors' Saloon of 1897 arrived on 3 October and remains a popular vehicle for private hire functions.

The new carriage shed under construction at Horsted Keynes in 1971.

The privately owned Great Northern Railway Directors' Saloon of 1897 arrived on 3 October 1971. (R. C. Riley)

1972

With a lack of necessary workshop facilities, Adams tank No. 488 goes to Swindon Works for overhaul.

The former W. H. Smith bookstall from Hassocks station is saved for preservation and removed 'flatpack' to Sheffield Park.

Bernard Holden takes up the full-time position of Superintendent of the Line in April.

Initial thoughts of 'breaking out' of the restrictive 5-mile line and extending north are made with an initially unsuccessful attempt to purchase trackbed north of Horsted Keynes.

The Bulleid Society's LSWR B4 Dock Tank No. 96 *Normandy* arrives on 19 December.

LSWR B4 Dock Tank No. 96 *Normandy* arrives on 19 December 1972.

1973

The field north of Station Approach at Horsted Keynes is purchased for £2,900 at the Highbrook Estate auction.

An appeal is launched for a locomotive workshop. No. 488 returns from Swindon and enters traffic on 4 August, whilst the wheelsets from C Class No. 592 are sent to Hunslet of Leeds for repair.

The stanchions and canopy support awnings from the demolished Hassocks station are purchased for eventual use at Horsted Keynes platforms 1 and 2.

The 1970s became a popular decade for filming TV advertisements, classic comedies and films depicting classics of literature on location at the railway.

Stephen Lewis (Inspector Blake) is left dangling from the parapets of Sloop Bridge having travelled on an open-top bus in the *On the Omnibuses* film for television.

1974

Ken Russell was one of the most controversial film directors of the 1960s and 1970s and four of his most celebrated films – *Savage Messiah*, *Mahler*, *Tommy* and *Lisztomania* – had the railway as a background and featured Bluebell volunteers as extras.

Horsted Keynes became Vocklabruck for Ken Russell's film *Mahler*, released in 1974.

Fenchurch bears down on a grand piano constructed of balsa wood and primed with explosives for Ken Russell's film *Lisztomania*.

1975

The railway celebrates its fifteenth anniversary and construction starts on a new locomotive workshop. At Horsted Keynes the end of Station Approach, by the station house, is breached and the roadway extended into the field (purchased in 1973) to become a car park/picnic area/events field.

Nationally, the 'Stockton & Darlington 150' celebration event at Shildon dominates the headlines. Bluebell sends locomotive *Fenchurch* and an LBSCR wagon to take part in the cavalcade.

Fenchurch and its famous 'whitewashed coal' at the 1975 exhibition and cavalcade to mark the 150th anniversary of the Stockton & Darlington Railway in 1825.

A poster announcing the railway's firm intentions, published at the time of the extended mortgage on the West Hoathly site in 1975.

Despite not owning any trackbed, the former station site at West Hoathly comes on to the market and an appeal for funds is made and the site secured for the future, in order to stop any housing development blocking the route forever.

1976

The year started on the wrong foot, with an initial request for planning permission to build a railway from Horsted Keynes to West Hoathly being rejected by Mid Sussex District Council by three votes to two with two abstentions on 21 January. A day later, SECR H Class No. 263 arrives from Ashford, owned by the H Class Trust.

Construction of a new purpose-built brick bookshop begins on the Down platform at Sheffield Park, while the former ex-Hassocks W. H. Smith bookstall is moved to its final position on Horsted Keynes platforms.

15–16 May was the 'big weekend' for the Bulleid Society with the return to steam after overhaul of No. 21C123 *Blackmoor Vale*, looking resplendent with a rake of overhauled matching Bulleid coaches.

It's the year of the heatwave and several fires are caused by locomotive cinders in adjacent fields and woodland through the school summer holidays.

Autumn sees the first 'Starlight Special' train. The novelty of a train running 'after dark', with a barbeque at Horsted Keynes, runs for several years.

The ex-Hassocks W. H. Smith bookstall moves to its permanent position at Horsted Keynes.

SR No. 21C123 *Blackmoor Vale* is restored to traffic. (Phil Barnes)

Blackmoor Vale waits to have its nameplate unveiled by artist David Shepherd on 15 May 1976.

U class No. 1618, partially repainted in BR black livery having run in SR livery since its arrival in 1977.

1977

The owners of SR U class No. 1618 bring their locomotive to the Bluebell Railway after finding it too heavy to be used on the Kent & East Sussex Railway.

On 15 May SR Bulleid Q1 class Austerity locomotive No. C1 (33001) arrives at Bluebell on loan from the National Collection and was a popular locomotive on the line prior to returning to York in 2004 as an example of a wartime constructed engine for Railfest, York.

A fund is launched to purchase BR Standard Class 4 tank No. 80100 from Barry Scrapyard as an example of a class that was closely associated with the last years of the line under British Railways. In 2019 it remains stored in ex-Barry Scrapyard condition.

1978

The LBSCR timber waiting room from the Down platform at Isfield is dismantled and moved to Sheffield Park Up platform. Initially planned as a guards' mess room, it then housed a model railway and now serves as the Bulleid Shop, raising funds for locomotives *Blackmore Vale* and *Sir Archibald Sinclair*.

A water crane from Clapham Junction yard is removed to Sheffield Park yard.

A further planning application is made to Mid Sussex District Council to extend the railway from Horsted Keynes station to East Grinstead station. Permission was refused by just one vote and thus preparations were begun for a public inquiry to appeal against the decision.

BR Standard class 9F locomotive No. 92240 arrives at the railway, funded by members' donations. SR S15 class No. 847 and SR Q class No. 541 also arrive in October (the Maunsell Locomotive Society is formed), as does BR Standard Class 4 tank No. 80100.

On the coaching front, SR Post Office Sorting Car No. 4922 arrives, along with LSWR Lavatory Brake Third No. 1520.

Above left: SR Post Office Sorting Car No. 4922 in 'as arrived' condition.

Above right: LSWR Lavatory Brake Third No. 1520, which had previously been used as a mobile first aid coach.

1979

A new running shed is under construction, providing undercover storage for locomotives, although it would be many years before the westernmost wall was completed.

Fingall – the railway's first Pullman Car – arrives on 27 June, followed by SR Bulleid 'Battle of Britain' Class Pacific No. 34059 *Sir Archibald Sinclair*. BR Standard Class 5 No. 73082 *Camelot* arrives, owned by the 73082 Camelot Locomotive Society.

Rescued in 1979 from Barry Scrapyard, 'Battle of Britain' Class Pacific No. 34059 *Sir Archibald Sinclair* returned to service in April 2009 but regrettably was withdrawn two years later for further firebox repairs. Work is currently progressing on its return to traffic.

The twentieth anniversary birthday cake, 2 August 1980. (R. C. Riley)

1980

The railway celebrates its twentieth anniversary and the BRPS hosts a twenty-first anniversary exhibition.

An appeal is launched to bring the remains of BR Standard Class 2MT No. 78059 to the railway from Barry Scrapyard to recreate 2MT tank locomotive No. 84030, a type that never made it to preservation.

SR V 'Schools' Class No. 928 *Stowe* arrives from the East Somerset Railway.

The NRM's Q1 class Austerity locomotive No. C1 (33001) enters traffic.

1981

The heavy engineering project to lay a scissors crossover point is completed adjacent to the locomotive yard at Sheffield Park.

'Schools' Class No. 928 *Stowe* returns to traffic and a redundant former LBSCR goods shed from Three Bridges arrives at Horsted Keynes.

During November, the steam-operated 45-ton Ransomes & Rapier breakdown crane arrives at the line from Newton Heath, Manchester, at a cost of £6,250.

Above left: The steam crane arrives on the line in 1981. It would take part in the line centenary cavalcade a year later.

Above right: TV personality and Bluebell Vice President Johnny Morris with Line Superintendent Bernard Holden in 1981.

1982

The year is dominated by the centenary of the line celebrations, being opened in 1882. A cavalcade of locomotives is held in June and the NRM's non-operational exhibit LBSCR locomotive *Gladstone* pays a visit.

A second Pullman Car, *Bertha*, arrives, along with Manning Wardle No. 4 of 1877 *Sharpthorn* – a historically important locomotive used on the construction of the Lewes to East Grinstead line by contractor Joseph Firbank. Note the spelling of the loco's name differs from the modern spelling used for Sharpthorne village.

Tentative steps are taken to provide higher quality evening dining trains with the launch of the 'Bluebell Cutler', utilising normal passenger stock such as SR Open Third No. 1309.

A redundant footbridge at Lingfield station is identified as being ideal for Sheffield Park as it has a double-width platform, designed for racegoers.

Fenchurch is 'christened' in style as it re-enters traffic at the line centenary in 1982.

LBSCR locomotives *Fenchurch* and *Gladstone* on shed at Sheffield Park in August 1982.

Above left: Adams tank No. 30583 and *Stepney* head a 'Poppy Day Special' in 1982. (R. C. Riley)

Above right: The redundant double-width racegoers' footbridge at Lingfield is identified as being ideal for Sheffield Park.

1983

The long-awaited public inquiry against the extension planning refusal takes place on 21 June at Oaklands, Haywards Heath. The railway still only owned the former station site at West Hoathly but options to purchase land at New Coombe Farm and Ingwersens, signed that very morning, were handed to the inspector.

The railway's first former LBSCR passenger coach arrives, being the remains of No. 661, which were incorporated into a bungalow at Bracklesham Bay. The restored coach entered traffic in 2004.

The centenary of the Ardingly branch is commemorated with a BRPS-chartered Western Region Class 119 DMU 'Ardingly 100' Special from Haywards Heath to Ardingly and back.

SR Q class No. 541 returns to traffic in November.

Five shuttles were run from Haywards Heath to Ardingly on 3 September 1993 for the 'Ardingly 100' centenary event. One is seen approaching Copyhold Junction in the hands of Class 119 DMU No. L 582. (Phil Barnes)

1984

Kingscote station comes on to the open market – an appeal fund is launched to purchase it for a price 'in excess of £100,000' with contracts exchange in 1985.

BR Standard Class 4MT No. 80064 arrives on 28 May, owned by a group based at the Dart Valley Railway, and immediately works out the remainder of its boiler certificate. No. 323 *Bluebell* goes to the East Somerset Railway on loan.

The North London Railway tank locomotive enters traffic and a fund is launched to purchase Pullman Car No. 54.

Kingscote station, with its 'For Sale' board, in 1985.

Kingscote station at the time of its purchase in 1985.

The ticket office window at Kingscote had survived the various misguided modernisation attempts of previous owners.

1985

Following the 1983 public inquiry, the Secretary of State gives planning approval and a Light Railway Order for the northern extension.

Saviour of the Bluebell line Miss Bessemer dies, aged eighty-seven, on 21 April.

The railway celebrates its silver jubilee with a gala in August.

The steam crane enters service, the S&T Department completes its major project to build the Sheffield Park Inner Home bracket signal and 'The Kingscote Club' (later to become Friends of Kingscote) makes a start on restoring Kingscote station.

The ex-Lingfield footbridge is erected at Sheffield Park, making it safer for visitors to cross platforms. Mk 1 RMB No. 1818 arrives and the mortgage on the West Hoathly site is paid off. SR carriage No. 1309 wins the ARPS Coach of the Year award.

A special meeting is held to allow the railway's operating arm, Bluebell Rly Ltd, to become Bluebell Rly plc – thus paving the way to launch a fundraising share issue – and the Bluebell Trust (the charitable arm of the railway) is founded.

The railway celebrates its silver jubilee with a gala in August 1985. *Fenchurch* and No. 541 double-head a train north on 26 August. (Phil Barnes)

The ex-Lingfield footbridge is erected at Sheffield Park.

The buffet at Sheffield Park, built in 1986.

The redundant cabin from Brighton Upper Goods signal box comes to Sheffield Park.

1986

The first plc share issue is launched and the new buffet building at Sheffield Park is under construction and opens later in the year.

The uppermost timber section of the redundant Brighton Upper Goods signal box arrives at Sheffield Park.

With the increasing operation of trains after dark, the oil-fired platform lamps at Sheffield Park are converted to gas light.

700 metres of track north of West Hoathly are purchased and LSWR B4 No. 96 *Normandy* returns to traffic.

1987

A former Great Northern Railway Atlantic locomotive boiler is found at an Essex laundry. It provides the impetus to launch a new-build LBSCR Atlantic project and the boiler arrives at Sheffield Park on 12 September. The loco workshop receives an overhead crane.

The Stepney Club is launched for children up to eight years old.

A suitable replacement deck for the missing bridge at New Coombe, just north of West Hoathly, is sourced from the A55 North Wales road improvement scheme and two of the spans arrive at Horsted Keynes.

British Rail announces electrification of the route from South Croydon to East Grinstead, thus securing the long-term future of the line north of our proposed terminus.

On 19 September ED Class 73 locomotive No. 73004 is named *The Bluebell Railway* at East Grinstead station.

Hurricane-force winds of the Great Storm on the night of 15/16 October fell many trees across Sussex, blocking off local villages with several trees felled across the railway's tracks.

Pullman Car No. 64 arrives at the railway and the trackbed from Horsted Keynes to Horsted House Farm and immediately north (260 metres) and south (130 metres) of Kingscote are purchased.

A suitable replacement deck for the missing bridge at New Coombe is sourced from this A55 North Wales road improvement scheme.

ED Class 73 locomotive No. 73004 is named *The Bluebell Railway* at East Grinstead station on 19 September 1987, with Johnny Morris, Bernard Holden and Gordon Pettitt.

The trackbed from Horsted Keynes to Horsted House Farm is purchased in 1987. The bridge at this location is seen here, still with its brick wall from its previous incarnation as a firing range.

1988

Physical progress on the northern extension begins on 13 March with the ceremonial laying of the first section of track at Leamland by the Rt Hon. Paul Channon MP, Secretary of State for Transport.

The first share issue closes at £461,630, enabling extension land purchases to be negotiated.

The 'Bluebell Cutler' dining train is renamed 'The Regency Belle' and Pullman Car No. 64 makes its debut.

Owned by Southern Locomotives Ltd, SR 'Merchant Navy' class No. 35027 *Port Line* arrives on 31 May (and leaves in early 2000). *Port Line* and B4 No. 96 *Normandy* attend Eastleigh Open Day on 18 September.

The ceremonial laying of the first track panel on the northern extension on 13 March 1988.

The track panel is nearly in place, with the aid of the steam crane.

Looking south at Horsted House Farm, with farm building and animal pens still *in situ* on the trackbed.

A fundraising sponsored walk starts from Kingscote station on 24 June 1989.

1989

Tracklaying progresses from Leamland Bridge to Horsted House Farm Bridge and the grounded body of LBSCR Bogie First No. 142 (SR No. 7598) arrives from West Chiltington, where it had stood since 1931 as a domestic dwelling and latterly as an aviary.

The volunteer group Friends of Kingscote is launched, replacing the Kingscote Club and establishes a base at our northern outpost to restore the station. The Brighton Upper Goods signal cabin is earmarked for Kingscote and it moves north from Sheffield Park.

1990

The railway celebrates thirty years of operations with an 'extension shuttle' – operating independently from the rest of the railway from Platform 1 at Horsted Keynes – running a mile northwards to Horsted House Farm. The novelty of running a first 'non-stop train' through Horsted Keynes for twenty-nine years is a sell-out.

An extension is added to the locomotive works and the restored BR 9F No. 92240 enters traffic, becoming the first of the ex-Barry 9Fs to be restored to traffic.

The first shuttle train on the Easter opening day arrives at the buffer stops at Horsted House Farm, the bridge still being half bricked up at this point.

The 'extension shuttle' consisted of No. 323 *Bluebell* with carriages No. 1309 and No. 6575, the latter being modified at the north end to facilitate the propelled train.

A second share issue is launched, primarily for continuing the construction of the railway from New Coombe Bridge to Kingscote. ED No 73004's *The Bluebell Railway* nameplate and crest is transferred to 'Dutch' liveried classmate No. 73133.

1991

The trackbed north of Horsted House Farm to Sharpthorne tunnel is cleared and prepared for tracklaying. At 731 yards, the tunnel is the longest on a UK heritage railway.

The 'Golden Arrow' Pullman premium dining train is launched, utilising Pullman Cars *Bertha* and Car No. 64.

Locomotive No. 55 *Stepney* attends the 'Brighton Line 150' celebrations at Brighton station.

Horsted Keynes becomes Churston for *The ABC Murders* – the first of many filming visits to the railway through the 1990s from David Suchet as Poirot.

The fencing gang at work at the south end of Sharpthorne Tunnel in February 1991.

David Suchet (Hercule Poirot) and Hugh Fraser (Captain Hastings) at Horsted Keynes.

1992

B4 No. 96 *Normandy* heads the first engineers' train through Sharpthorne Tunnel in March to the site of West Hoathly station, followed by the 'official opening' of the tunnel on 16 May.

A group is formed to start restoration of the 'long out-of-traffic' set of four Metropolitan Railway carriages under the name of 'BASH' – Bluebell Ashbury Supporters & Helpers – and begins fundraising.

On 8 September, Network SouthEast hands the ownership of Imberhorne Viaduct to Bluebell for a token £1.00, which was paid for by company secretary John Potter.

A month later, Superintendent of the Line Bernard Holden receives an MBE for services to railway preservation.

Above left: B4 No. 96 *Normandy* heads the first engineers' train through Sharpthorne Tunnel in March 1992.

Above right: No. 35027 *Port Line* waits to break the banner for the official opening of the tunnel on 16 May 1992 at a ceremony performed by Sir Alastair Morton, chairman of Eurotunnel.

Bernard Holden MBE.

1993

The three sections of new decking at New Coombe Bridge are completed on 10 May at a cost of £43,000, saving £10,000 on the original estimate and a lot more if the job had gone to outside contract.

Trackbed clearance progresses a further 2 miles north to Kingscote and the extension engineers' base moves from its West Hoathly site to East Grinstead.

SR S15 class No. 847 returns to traffic.

Right: The final span is lifted into position at New Coombe Bridge on 10 May 1993.

Below: Adjustments to the bridge decking are underway on 22 May 1993.

1994

A milestone year for the railway with the opening of the new northern terminus at Kingscote. The first public passenger train to serve Kingscote arrived on 23 April, the 10 a.m. from Sheffield Park, hauled by SECR C class No. 592.

The 'official' opening of Kingscote station came on 21 May and No. 592 again did the honours, specially decorated in LBSCR floral style.

LSWR 'Greyhound' T9 No. 120 comes to the railway on 24 March on loan from the National Railway Museum and leaves on 1 February 2008.

LSWR B4 No. 96 *Normandy* visits its old stamping ground of Southampton Docks in June and the volunteer-led scheme to replace the missing canopy on the westernmost platforms at Horsted Keynes begins. The canopy had been removed in SR days to help the sighting of signals from the signalbox.

The first public train to Kingscote arrives on 23 April 1994.

C class No. 592 breaks the banner for the 'official' opening of Kingscote station on 21 May 1994.

LSWR B4 No. 96 *Normandy* visits Southampton Docks on 3 June 1994.

Iron spandrels and stanchions sprouting at Horsted Keynes, using materials saved from Hassocks and Lavant stations.

1995

The railway celebrates thirty-five years of operations, including a visit from SR No. 30777 *Sir Lamiel*.

A landslip at Black Hut curtails services from Sheffield Park to Horsted Keynes only.

The railway becomes a film set for three weeks with the major production of a new feature film version of the classic story *The Wind in the Willows*. It was directed by ex 'Python' Terry Jones who plays Toad, alongside Eric Idle (Ratty) and Steve Coogan (Mole).

Trustees and officers of the Bluebell Railway Preservation Society celebrate thirty-five years of operations on 5 August 1995.

The restored station at Kingscote in July 1995.

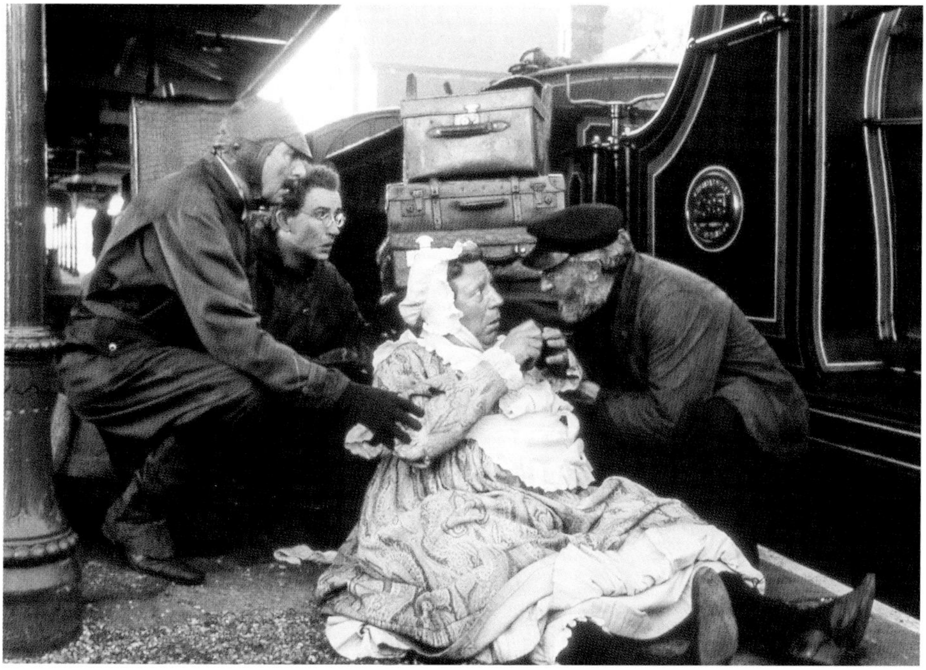

Wind in the Willows filming as Toad (Terry Jones) pleads with the engine driver to be let aboard.

Ratty and Mole (Eric Idle and Steve Coogan) are 'stranded' after a train-splitting scene in *Wind in the Willows*.

1996

The 'temporary' Kingscote South signal cabin opens, which allows two-train running to our northern outpost. Meanwhile the former Brighton Upper Goods signal box upper section gets lifted on to a new brick base at the north end of Kingscote's Down Platform, the site of the original signal box. Friends of Kingscote make a start on erecting the Down side canopy.

Having been the headquarters of the Bluebell's in-house fire department, a project to restore LSWR carriage No. 1520 to traffic as a wheelchair-accessible vehicle begins.

GWR No. 3217 *Earl of Berkeley* passes the temporary Kingscote South signal cabin.

The former Brighton Upper Goods signal box on its new brick base at Kingscote in July 1996.

LSWR 'mobile fire train' No. 1520, prior to stripping down to restore to its pre-Grouping splendour and to convert it to a disabled access vehicle.

Friends of Kingscote erecting canopy supports and back wall steelwork to the Down side canopy on 6 April 1996.

1997

The 1896 Ashford-built SER O1 class No. 65 arrives at the railway, having been obtained in 1963 by the late Esmond Lewis-Evans and kept at Ashford Steam Centre until its closure. It returned to steam at Bluebell two years later.

The railway acquires the former trackbed between Horsted Keynes and Ardingly from the Borde Hill Estate, thanks to a member's generosity. There are no current plans by Bluebell to re-lay track and operate on this section.

Pullman Car No. 76 is restored and renamed *Lilian*, after our President Bernard Holden MBE's wife.

The handsome lines of SER O1 class No. 65, which came to the railway in 1997 and returned to traffic in 1999, seen here in tandem with SECR C class No. 592.

The railway acquires the former trackbed between Horsted Keynes and Ardingly. Sherriff Mill Viaduct, just west of Horsted Keynes, was demolished in the mid-1960s.

The former station building at Ardingly is used by Hanson as offices.

1998

Privately owned BR Standard Class 4MT No. 80151 arrives at the line and the fortieth anniversary of the final line closure is commemorated in March. No. 80151 runs in the guise of No. 80154, which hauled the last passenger train on the line.

The board approves construction of an extension to the carriage shed, allowing five coaches to be worked on simultaneously.

The railway mourns the passing of 'Mr Extension', Peter Thomas OBE, who did so much behind the scenes to get the railway to Kingscote and lay the groundwork for the final push to East Grinstead.

LBSCR No. 473 *Birch Grove* is restored in time for its centenary in June, and No. 55 *Stepney* also returns to steam amid a hugely successful 'Thomas' weekend. The line's first wheelchair-accessible disabled coach, Mk 1 TSO No. 5034, enters traffic.

No. 80151 runs in the guise of No. 80154 for the fortieth anniversary of the final line closure, seen near Horsted House Farm with the 10.15 a.m. Kingscote to Sheffield Park on 14 March 1998. (Phil Barnes)

Disabled volunteer Dave Deeks demonstrates the wheelchair lift at the commissioning of access vehicle No. 5034.

1999

The first two of the Metropolitan Railway coaches, Nos 387 and 394, enter traffic with No. 387 winning the Transport Trust's Peter Allen Award. LBSCR Bogie First (SR No. 5768) enters traffic on 30 May.

The first two of the Metropolitan Railway coaches, Nos 387 and 394, enter traffic, seen at the Winter Steam-Up on 13 February 1999. (Phil Barnes)

Jenny Agutter played 'mother' in the TV remake of *The Railway Children*, seen here with 'old gentleman' Richard Attenborough and the children.

Filming *The Railway Children* with the GNR saloon at the rear in the guise of the 'old gentleman's carriage'.

The North London Railway tank, in the guise of LMS No. 27505, is loaned to Barrow Hill Roundhouse for two years. The 9F Club, for young people aged nine to sixteen, has a successful working year.

The Horsted Keynes re-signalling scheme gets underway. 9,400 visitors flock to the 'Friends of Thomas' event and it's a big year for filming as Carlton TV takes over the railway in the autumn for a TV film remake of *The Railway Children.*

2000

The fortieth anniversary year kicks off with a Founder Members' Day on 17 May and a Summer Steam Gala anniversary weekend on 5–6 August with Isle of Wight Railway visiting locos Nos W8 and W11.

Steam tram engine No. 18 *Leeghwater* visits from Stoomtram Hoorn Medemblik in Holland and Bulleids Nos 21C123 and 34081 double-head at the Giants of Steam event.

The carriage shed extension is completed externally and the LBSCR goods lock-up from the dock at Horsted Keynes goes to Kingscote goods yard.

The first two restored Metropolitan Railway coaches visit Rickmansworth for May's 'Steam on the Met' event.

Kingscote's down canopy back wall is completed and the last parcels of trackbed between Kingscote and East Grinstead are purchased.

Kingscote gets its first major filming role in *Station Jim*, a children's TV story about a railway dog, set in the Victorian era.

Steam tram engine No. 18 *Leeghwater* visits from Stoomtram Hoorn Medemblik in the Netherlands and is seen at Leamland Bridge in September 2000. (Phil Barnes)

The western extension to the carriage shed is externally complete in 2000.

The arrival of the Royal Train. No. 592, dressed with garlands of fresh hydrangeas and laurel, leaves for filming *Station Jim*.

Progress on the Horsted Keynes canopy project, with a roof at the southern end and brickwork for chimneys under construction.

2001

A major landslip severs the line at Ingwersens, south of Kingscote, while track clearance continues on the northern extension at Hazelden Farm.

Pullman Car No. 64 is overhauled and returned to traffic.

The annual Steam Fair is cancelled and lineside passes revoked, due to nationwide Foot and Mouth precautions.

BR Standard 4MT No. 80151 steams again for the first time in thirty-four years.

Trustees report the opportunity to purchase 'all or part' of the land adjoining the west of Sheffield Park station – the 'Woodpax' site. Donations and loans are sought from members to purchase enough land to hopefully build a carriage stock 'running shed'.

The restored BR 4MT No. 80151, steaming again after thirty-four years.

A public open day allows visitors to see ongoing maintenance work on the parapets of Imberhorne Viaduct.

2002

Bluebell is officially twinned with Stoomtram Hoorn Medemblik in The Netherlands at a ceremony at Hoorn on 20 May in the company of No. 672 *Fenchurch*.

The third Metropolitan Railway coach, No. 368, is completed.

The railway receives its first official royal visit as it welcomes Princess Alexandra to Sheffield Park on 17 July.

Maintenance continues on Imberhorne Viaduct and the board approves plans for a new shop at Sheffield Park.

BRPS chairman Roy Watts confirms the official twinning arrangement with his Dutch counterpart – Jaap Nieweg of Stoomtram Hoorn Medemblik.

The way north at Hazelden, as the trackbed is cleared in the spring of 2002.

2003

The 'Woodpax' site for building a carriage running shed and new museum is secured, helped by members who raised £375,000 towards the project.

LBSCR Bogie First carriage No. 7598 wins Best Coach in the Heritage Railway Association Awards for 2002/3.

Construction work on the new shop premises at Sheffield Park starts on 27 May.

Tracklaying north of Kingscote station towards Imberhorne begins, with the first section of track laid in the presence of the Mayor of East Grinstead on 29 October.

GWR No. 9017 returns to traffic, following overhaul.

Trackbed clearance north of Kingscote at 'Browns', looking south towards Kingscote station.

The steel framework for the new shop and office building is underway at Sheffield Park.

The new shop is under construction and the days are numbered for the old single-storey shop building, seen behind.

2004

At a cost of some £350,000, the new shop and office accommodation at Sheffield Park opens in May.

Tracklaying is completed to the southern end of the tip.

LBSCR Stroudley First Class coach No. 661 returns to traffic on 24 July, following restoration from 'bungalow status' at Bracklesham Bay.

The 'Woodpax' scheme to build a new carriage running shed and museum receives a Stage 1 Heritage Lottery Fund pass.

Horsted Keynes station receives a special National Railway Heritage twenty-fifth anniversary award.

A new shop with office accommodation above opens in May 2004 at Sheffield Park.

Another vintage carriage that saw a new life as part of a domestic dwelling after railway service is back on the rails and restored to traffic – LBSCR Stroudley First Class coach No. 661.

Horsted Keynes station receives a special National Railway Heritage twenty-fifth anniversary award.

2005

Society membership breaks through the 9,000 barrier.

Monday 6 June becomes 'D-Day' on the northern extension, with the beginning of special trains to remove the clay capping at the southern end of Imberhorne Tip, utilising on-loan Ivatt tank locomotive No. 41312. A hundred train movements are required to move the spoil, which is being hauled to fill in the formation of the Ardingly Spur at Horsted Keynes. Imberhorne Lane Bridge then becomes exposed, having been 'buried' since the cutting was filled with waste.

Brighton Box Van No. 8196 receives the Heritage Railway Association's carriage and wagon award.

'Nibbling the elephant' – the operation to remove the clay capping of the tip at Imberhorne Lane Bridge, utilising visiting Ivatt engine No. 41312.

Two wagons of clay capping at Kingscote en route to the Ardingly spur at Horsted Keynes.

Looking south, with the removal of the clay capping, Imberhorne Lane Bridge is exposed again after decades of being 'buried'.

2006

The west wall of the locomotive running shed is finally completed, twenty-seven years after the remaining structure was built!

The volunteer-led project to reconstruct the buildings and canopy on platforms 1 and 2 at Horsted Keynes is completed.

Old promises are 'settled' when the railway concludes purchase of part of the former East Grinstead goods yard from Network Rail for its northern terminus platform.

The last of the four Metropolitan Railway coaches is completed and SR Maunsell locomotive No. 1638 returns to steam.

LCDR coach No. 114 is restored to service, which was encased within a bungalow at Bosham for fifty years.

The Bluebell Museum receives full registration status and the Brighton Atlantic new-build scheme opens its new workshop headquarters. Trackbed clearance continues in the cutting south of Imberhorne Lane Bridge.

The running shed west wall is completed at Sheffield Park, to emulate that at Tunbridge Wells West.

Atlantic House workshop opens, with a donor presenting the original regulator handle from Brighton Atlantic No. 32424 *Beachy Head*.

The buildings and canopies on platforms 1 and 2 at Horsted Keynes were completed in 2006.

2007

Pullman Car *Christine* is launched into traffic and the rake of Metropolitan Railway coaches receive the outright winners award at the Heritage Railway Association's carriage and wagon competition.

The contract for Imberhorne Cutting to pass to Bluebell ownership from West Sussex County Council is signed for a 'mere' £6,000 plus legal fees.

The railway purchases former BR 4VEP electric unit No. 3417 for a nominal £1 from owners SouthWest Trains.

A LEGR 125 event gala runs on 10–11 August, marking the 125th anniversary of the opening of the line.

Bluebell stations are marked on the official East Grinstead version of the popular board game Monopoly.

The completed rake of Metropolitan Railway coaches receives the outright winners' award at the 2007 Heritage Railway Association's carriage and wagon competition.

Imberhorne Tip is purchased from West Sussex County Council for £6,000, and is viewed here on 5 June 2007.

Seen at Eastleigh, BR 4VEP electric unit No. 3417 is purchased by the railway for a nominal £1.00.

2008

The Heritage Lottery Fund awards the railway £2.85 million to build a carriage stock running shed on the 'Woodpax' land at Sheffield Park and rebuild the adjoining museum into a twenty-first-century attraction.

BRPS membership passes the 10,000 barrier for the first time and the railway passes the £3 million turnover mark.

The clearance of vegetation on top of Imberhorne Tip is completed.

A third share offer of £670,000 is launched to help purchase the tip and remaining land. There are 300,000 cubic metres of waste to be removed.

On 25 November, in the presence of the media, the first ground-breaking 'dig' at Imberhorne Tip begins. Diggers lift the waste into lorries for onward journey to landfill. In the event, 15,000 tons of waste left by road.

The three share issues, launched in 1986, 1991 and 2008, did much to raise funds towards the Northern Extension Project.

The media and invited guests await the 'first dig' of Imberhorne Tip on 25 November 2008.

The first dig at Imberhorne Lane Bridge where, much to the delight of onlookers, the first 'scoop-full' included a pair of trousers!

2009

4VEP unit No. 3417 *Gordon Pettitt* is officially passed to Bluebell ownership from SouthWest Trains in a ceremony at East Grinstead station to mark the physical connection of the Bluebell to the main network.

Track is beginning to be laid from East Grinstead to the northern end of the tip, which will pave the way for removing the tip spoil northwards by rail, whilst at the south end of the tip, the spoil capping is gradually removed at Imberhorne Lane Bridge for transport to the 'Ardingly Triangle' at Horsted Keynes.

BR No. 34059 *Sir Archibald Sinclair* returns to traffic, while the 4VEP unit and B4 loco No. 96 *Normandy* travel to Eastleigh for the works centenary celebrations. 'Tenner for the Tip' scheme is launched as a cost-effective way of soliciting donations from passengers and supporters. A C&W public viewing area opens as a grant of £49,500 is awarded by the 'People's Millions' Lottery Fund to make LCDR coach No. 51 disabled-access friendly.

4VEP unit No. 3417 *Gordon Pettitt* arrives at East Grinstead to mark the handover to Bluebell ownership and the physical connection of Bluebell metals to the national network.

BR No. 34059 *Sir Archibald Sinclair* returns to traffic, seen working a special on 21 April 2009.

2010

The fiftieth anniversary year kicks off with *Birch Grove* returning to traffic as B473 and track is relaid on Imberhorne Viaduct and pointwork on the station throat at East Grinstead. The trial removal of the tip waste by rail in July is a success.

BRPS volunteers win the Queen's Award for Voluntary Service – the first railway preservation group to receive such an award.

A successful anniversary gala is followed by the opening of East Grinstead station to visitors on 4 September, allowing visitors to travel to the tip face at Imberhorne North with 4VEP unit No. 3417 *Gordon Pettitt* hauled by 73208 *Kirsten*.

6 November – history is made with the first 'through train' to Bluebell metals since 1963, when Hastings DEMU No. 1001 comes from London Bridge down to East Grinstead and down to the tip face.

The C&W Dept adds a Sentinel diesel shunter to its stock.

The fiftieth anniversary locomotive cavalcade at Horsted Keynes, August 2010. (Phil Barnes)

Fiftieth anniversary crowds enjoy the spectacle.

East Grinstead station opens to visitors for the first time on 4 September 2010.

2011

The 'Waste by Rail' activity continues at Imberhorne Cutting, with diggers placing spoil into wagons for removal north by rail – each full wagon load train costs £24,000.

P Class No. 323 *Bluebell* is restored to traffic and SECR No. 3360 enters traffic.

Lord Faulkner of Worcester opens the new museum at Sheffield Park on 23 June and rails are laid into the new 'Woodpax' carriage shed.

The Friends of Sheffield Park group is formed to look after the station's infrastructure.

Downton Abbey fever comes to Horsted Keynes – the ITV drama being one of the most popular TV series of the year. The station becomes Downton village for filming in 2011 and 2012.

No. 66743 takes a wagonload of spoil from Imberhorne Tip to East Grinstead and on to landfill at Bedford, passing Hill Place Farm on 14 July 2011.

Horsted Keynes becomes 'Downton' for filming the popular TV drama series *Downton Abbey*.

2012

A further fundraising campaign is initiated in March to raise £100,000 to finish the Northern Extension Project – £200,000 is raised in six days!

90,000 tons of waste is removed northwards by rail from Imberhorne Cutting before the end of the Landfill Tax Exemption. Tracklaying begins to bridge the 'gap' through the cutting.

The entrance porch at Horsted Keynes is returned to the stained glass style of the Victorian original as-built condition, funded by members as a memorial to the late Simon Baker, who died in 2009.

The historic Furness Railway locomotive No. 20 visits the railway in connection with filming for Charles Dickins' *The Invisible Woman*.

The Kingscote Yard Project receives a boost as public services repair provider Mears brings materials and its apprentices to construct cattle pens on the dock.

Bernard Holden MBE – the 'founding father of standard gauge railway preservation' and Bluebell president – dies on 4 October, aged 104, and a start is made on constructing improved loco staff facilities above the workshop.

The final track alignment north of Imberhorne is in place, there having previously been double track at this location to enable the 'Waste by Rail' operation.

A thirty-wagon train containing 800 tons of fresh ballast arrives at East Grinstead on 28 November 2012, bound for the works at Imberhorne.

The entrance porch at Horsted Keynes is returned to its full Victorian splendour.

2013

A symbolic 'golden spike' ceremony for extension workers is held on 8 March at Imberhorne Lane Bridge, physically connecting the 'two railways'.

Following a series of test trains, public services return to East Grinstead for the opening gala on 23 March – the end of the forty-one-year project to extend to East Grinstead – amid blizzard conditions!

A consortium of Loco Dept members bring diesel-electric shunter D4106 to the railway on 23 April and Hollywood comes to Bluebell with the filming of Walt Disney's *Muppets Most Wanted* movie.

GBRf No. 66739 is named *Bluebell Railway* at a ceremony at Horsted Keynes in August.

A 'golden spike' ceremony is held on 8 March 2013 at Imberhorne Lane Bridge, connecting the 'two railways'.

Amid blizzard conditions, Bluebell's first public train arrives at East Grinstead on the gala opening day of 23 March 2013.

Crowds at East Grinstead on opening day.

Captain Baxter goes 'Wild West' and becomes Randy Stevenot for the *Muppets Most Wanted* movie – a most unlikely location for a Walt Disney extravaganza.

2014

The railway receives the 'Heritage Railway of the Decade' award, from the National Railway Heritage Awards scheme.

Pullman Car *Fingall* is outshopped after a rebuild, its second in Bluebell ownership, and a water tower is constructed at East Grinstead.

The Horsted Keynes resignalling scheme is completed and catering turnover tops £1 million for the first time. Chairman Roy Watts receives an MBE for 'services to the heritage railway movement and preservation'. An autumn appeal is made for 'Cash for Cover' to erect a new carriage shed at Horsted Keynes and raises £350,000 in just one month.

Pullman Car *Fingall* is outshopped after its second rebuild in Bluebell ownership.

The Horsted Keynes resignalling scheme is completed.

A brick water tower facility is constructed at East Grinstead station.

2015

A disabled toilet and platform canopy are constructed at East Grinstead.

Q Class No. 30541 and No. 73082 *Camelot* return to traffic.

The Friends of Sheffield Park complete the restoration of the entrance porch to original LBSCR condition.

Preserved 'Hastings' DEMU No. 1001 arrives at Sheffield Park on 25 September, the first of its type to travel the full length of the line, in connection with a member's private charter.

SECR Birdcage Brake No. 3363 wins the 2015 Heritage Railway Association 'Best Coach' award.

A disabled toilet and platform canopy are constructed on the platform at East Grinstead.

The stained glass of the entrance porch at Sheffield Park, reconstructed to original LBCSR condition.

'Hastings' DEMU No. 1001 traverses the full line for the first time on 25 September 2015.

SECR Birdcage Brake No. 3363 wins the 2015 Heritage Railway Association 'Best Coach' award.

2016

SECR No. 592 and eight carriages leave the railway top and tailed by two Class 20 locomotives for Bounds Green depot, in order to run into King's Cross in connection with a filming project.

Kingscote signal box is commissioned on 15 February.

The Heritage Lottery Fund confirms its £1.1 million support for the 'Accessible Steam Heritage' Project to replace the life-expired running shed roof, create a new visitor entrance and build a locomotive maintenance shed.

Rebuilt four-wheeler SECR carriage No. 3188 is launched to traffic after eighty years as part of a domestic dwelling in Devon and the Department for Transport makes an award of £75,000 towards restoration of Pullman Brake No. 54 as an accessible vehicle.

The novel sight of SECR C Class No. 592 and Bluebell carriages at King's Cross station in connection with a filming contract.

Kingscote signal box and its miniature levers are commissioned for traffic in February 2015.

An artist's impression of the Heritage Lottery-funded scheme to make the running shed engines accessible to those in wheelchairs.

The Department for Transport make an award of £75,000 towards the restoration of Pullman Brake No. 54 as an accessible vehicle.

2017

Network Rail clears gauging issues at Dormans station in readiness for the Easter week first-time visit of famous locomotive No. 60103 *Flying Scotsman* to the railway. 'Scotsman fever' is hailed a six-figure revenue success.

Carriage repairs benefit from the hardstanding maintenance road in the new carriage shed and the first of the twenty-five planned arrivals enter the new carriage shed.

SECR O1 No. 65 returns to traffic and the 'Elephant Van' childrens' play van project at Horsted Keynes, funded by an Arts Council England grant, opens in August.

The railway successfully hosts the Deltic Preservation Society's fortieth anniversary weekend on 6–8 October, with D9009 *Alycidon*, D9002 *The King's Own Yorkshire Light Infantry* and 55019 *Royal Highland Fusilier* in attendance.

The first of the successful *Flying Scotsman* trains was a breakfast Pullman service, which was 'piped out' from Sheffield Park.

'Scotsman Fever' at Sheffield Park.

Flying Scotsman with *Typhoon* from the Romney Hythe & Dymchurch Railway in Sheffield Park yard.

BR(S) Scenery 'Elephant Van' No. 4601 is restored as a 'play van' for young children at Horsted Keynes, thanks to an £84,150 grant from the Arts Council Museum Resilience Fund.

Deltic locomotives take over at Horsted Keynes on 6 October 2017. (Phil Barnes)

2018

Special trains are run on Friday 16 March then 17–18 March to mark the final BR train over the line sixty years ago. Invited guests include those that travelled on the last train, thinking that that would be the end of it all!

The Friends of Sheffield Park complete their LBSCR-style canopy around the Bessemer Arms, part of the original plan when the buffet was built.

A children's play area opens at Kingscote and the new lottery-funded SteamWorks! exhibition opens on 19 October in the loco running shed.

A public appeal is launched to raise funding for completing the walls to the new carriage shed at Horsted Keynes and to start construction of the adjacent Heritage Skills Centre.

Life member Clive Gobel brings his original smokebox numberplate from the last locomotive to traverse the line, sixty years ago. Clive's grandfather was a porter at Sheffield Park. The 'Victory' wreath carried on the last train is also replicated.

With special headboard, No. 541 approaches Imberhorne Lane on 18 March 2018.

The completed canopy at the Bessemer Arms.

The SteamWorks! exhibition at Sheffield Park opens to visitors.

2019

A celebratory dinner is held at Meridian Hall, East Grinstead, on 15 March to mark sixty years to the day that the Lewes & East Grinstead Railway Preservation Society was formed in 1959.

A new locomotive maintenance shed opens at Sheffield Park on the site of the railway's first loco shed, as part of the lottery-funded Steamworks! project.

The Metropolitan coaches go by rail to London to take part in what will probably be the last 'steam on the Underground' as part of the 'District Line 150' celebrations.

Development continues on the new carriage shed at Horsted Keynes, with cladding to the walls and completion of associated trackwork in the Down yard.

A celebratory dinner is held in East Grinstead on 15 March 2019 to mark sixty years to the day that the preservation society was formed in 1959.

The new locomotive maintenance shed at Sheffield Park.

SECR No. 65 is the first engine to make use of the new maintenance shed, which includes a pit road.

After many years being completely rebuilt, the Bulleid Society's CK No. 5768 returns to traffic.

Metropolitan Railway No. 1 hauls the Bluebell's rake of Metropolitan Railway coaches at the 'District Line 150' celebrations in London.

Support rails for the external cladding have been fitted, and perimeter walls for the new Heritage Skills Centre.

The ground floor of the Heritage Skills Centre with steel beams for the first floor.

An aerial view of the site, shortly after completion of the Heritage Skills Centre framework.

2020

The railway celebrates its diamond anniversary year with a host of special events, culminating in the sixtieth anniversary gala weekend on 7–9 August which includes 'Sixty things to see and do on the Bluebell Railway.'

Floreat Vapor!